28
2 70

Jennie Jenkins

Jennie Jenkins

by
Mark Taylor

Illustrated by
Glen Rounds

Little, Brown and Company
BOSTON   TORONTO

FIRST EDITION

T 04/75

Library of Congress Cataloging in Publication Data

Taylor, Mark.
    Jennie Jenkins.

    I. Rounds, Glen, 1906–   illus. II. Title.
PZ7.T2172Je   [Fic]   74-16155

ISBN 0-316-83357-6

Published simultaneously in Canada
by Little, Brown & Company (Canada) Limited

PRINTED IN THE UNITED STATES OF AMERICA

To Lois —
of all best friends, the best

I N TIMES 'way past and gone, there was a settlement called Nettle Bottom.

Not far from Nettle Bottom, up along Quicksand Branch, was the Jenkins place. It looked pretty battered and busted, but it could have looked worse.

There were lots of Jenkinses — seven people, three critters, and one *varmint*.

First off were Old Man Jenkins and Mizzus Jenkins. Old Man Jenkins didn't favor company and he hated strangers. But Mizzus

7

Jenkins favored whatever Old Man Jenkins didn't favor, so they spent all their time ripping into each other as to who would favor what.

The next four Jenkinses were Zeph, who was the oldest, and three grown-up daughters — Clara, Fannie, and Ida.

Then there was Jennie Jenkins. Now, Jennie was the youngest. She was also the smartest and the stubbornest. She had been born smart, but with three sisters to poke, pet, and pick on her, and one brother who liked to tease, Jennie had just naturally turned stubborn.

Jennie got along best with the three critters and the varmint. The three critters were two cows — Old Maudie and Young Maudie — and one mule called Poorly Jake because most times he felt too bad to work.

The varmint was a horse called Contraption. He was so ornery that nobody could hardly ever catch him and nobody at all could ride him — except Jennie.

Jennie's sisters each had a sweetheart. But their sweethearts were skitterish about asking them to marry. And since Clara, Fannie, and Ida were sort of prissy, nobody proposed to nobody.

"Pa just ought to send 'em packin'," Jennie told Zeph. "They aren't good for much. Primpin' themselves and makin' dreamy eyes at menfolk is all they know how to do."

Zeph laughed. "All young ladies can't do like you, Jennie. You're the only gal I know who can plow and hoe and help with hayin', dig 'taters, milk a cow, chop wood, hitch a team, and ride Contraption!"

"Well, that don't make me a freak — does it?" Then Jennie would get mad, and when she got mad she would redden in the face and stomp around, muttering under her breath. Zeph called it "rolling" when she did that, and he would say to her, "Roll, Jennie Jenkins, roll!"

11

Now, trouble began for Jennie when the folks in Nettle Bottom decided to have a big dance in the schoolhouse. It was the very first Nettle Bottom Ball.

Jennie's sisters were all set to go with their sweethearts. For days they giggled and gossiped about what to wear. Mizzus Jenkins fussed right along with them because she was going to be a chaperone.

"I do wish one of you girls could snag Brute Smith for a beau," she would sometimes sigh.

"Brute Smith's a man's man!" Old Man Jenkins would snort. "I reckon he can do better than get hitched to Clara, Fannie, or Ida."

"Pa! that's mean talk!" Mizzus Jenkins would scold. All the same, it was true. Brute Smith was the strongest, richest, handsomest young man in all the county. His real name was J. Brutus Smith, but they called him Brute. All the girls dreamed about him.

13

Jennie said the Nettle Bottom Ball was
the dumbest thing she'd ever heard about.
"If I was Brute, I wouldn't go to it," she
declared, "nor am *I* goin' to it neither!"

"Oh, but you *are* goin'," said Mizzus Jenkins. "It's time for you to be a young lady."

"We'll help you with your fixups," said
her sisters.

14

"I don't want to get gussied up and fussied up," Jennie argued, turning red.

But her sisters sniffed. "It's time you made yourself pretty and were a credit to us."

"I'm not pretty and I never will be pretty and I don't want to be *pretty!*" Jennie yelled as she stomped out of the house.

Zeph, his fiddle tucked under his arm, watched her go and grinned. He was going to be one of the fiddlers at the Ball. "Roll, Jennie Jenkins, roll!" he teased, and then he hummed a little tune.

Jennie kept on stomping off until she came to the field where Contraption was dozing under a tree.

"Yep," said Jennie to herself. "Those sisters will be sorry for what they're doin' to me. When I'm done, they won't have no sweethearts left, 'cause their sweethearts will

hate all Jenkinses. Then they won't go to no Ball, and neither will I!"

And with that, Jennie jumped up on Contraption and off she rode bareback to make her plans.

Each of Jennie's sisters saw their sweethearts on a different day. On Sundays Preacher Jeremiah came to dinner after church meeting. He was Sister Clara's sweetheart. When Sunday came, Jennie was ready for him.

After the meeting ended at the meetinghouse in Yonders Valley, Sister Clara and Jennie waited for Preacher Jeremiah to finish talking to a bunch of old ladies that always pestered him. Preacher Jeremiah always walked with the Jenkinses back to their house when the weather was right.

Pretty soon he came over to Clara and Jennie. He was young and tall and pale and thin, and most everybody said he was too good to be in this wicked world for very

long. Most of the time he did seem pretty wore out.

When Sister Clara wasn't looking, Jennie said, "Preacher, I'd like to do you a favor."

"A favor?" replied Preacher Jeremiah.

"Yep," said Jennie. "I can see you're tired from all that hard preaching this morning. I want to let you ride to our place on my horse Contraption."

Jennie led Preacher Jeremiah over to
where the varmint was hitched to a tree.
"Don't mind Contraption's steppin' around
some," she said. "He's just a mite spunky."

19

Well, no sooner did Preacher Jeremiah
settle down on Contraption's back than
Jennie let go the reins and Contraption shot
forward like a cannon going off! "Whoa!"
cried Preacher Jeremiah as he and Contraption disappeared through the trees.

That was the last they saw of Preacher
Jeremiah until they'd all rushed home and
found him lying flat on the ground by the
barn. Contraption stood nearby looking just
as peaceful as could be. But Sister Clara was

20

crying and hollering and calling out to Preacher Jeremiah, "Don't die, not yet!"

Preacher Jeremiah finally opened his eyes and smiled weakly at Sister Clara. "You're like an angel," he murmured. "Marry me."

"Oh, I will, I will!" cried Sister Clara.

"Drat!" muttered Jennie to herself. "He was supposed to hate us Jenkinses after that, not marry one of us."

Zeph nudged Jennie. "Some trick, Jennie, but who got fooled?" Then he hummed the tune Jennie had come to hate, and called "Roll, Jennie Jenkins, roll!" after her as she stomped away.

On Wednesdays Schoolmaster Tucker always came to supper and stayed late to spoon with Sister Fannie. People called him "Old Skinny Boney" behind his back, because he was so tall and thin. And since he couldn't see too well, even with eyeglasses, he was always stumbling over things, mostly his own two feet.

When Wednesday came, Jennie went out on the porch to wait for the schoolmaster. She had a little surprise for him. Pretty soon she saw him coming down the road. She held her breath until he got to the gate, which stood open. As soon as he walked through, Jennie hollered out, "Schoolmaster Tucker, will you kindly close the gate? Be sure to fix the latch."

Now none of the Jenkinses closed the gate because some wasps had built a big nest right by the latch. But the schoolmaster was nearsighted and didn't pay attention to things, and he did just what Jennie told him to do. He slammed the gate, pushed the latch hard, and broke open the wasps' nest.

23

In about fifteen seconds Schoolmaster
Tucker set up a yell and came running to
the porch with a cloud of crazy-mad wasps
following him. Jennie ducked inside.
Through the door the schoolmaster tore,
jumping up and down with the hurt of all
those stings.

24

That was some commotion! The Jenkinses had to get a few wasps out of the house. And then they had to tend to poor Schoolmaster Tucker, who was a sight! But Sister Fannie had an old-time remedy for wasp stings. After a couple hours the schoolmaster felt better. "Fannie," he said, "you just saved my life. Will you marry me?"

Old Man Jenkins cried, "Whoopee!" and Fannie said, "I will."

"Drat!" muttered Jennie.

Zeph whispered to Jennie, "And who got fooled this time?" Then, seeing Jennie turn red, he hummed his tune and sang softly, "Roll, Jennie Jenkins, roll!"

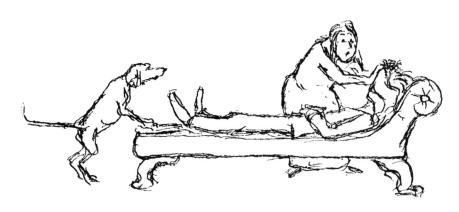

On Fridays Sister Ida's sweetheart, Mr.
Cooper, the storekeeper, came to call. He
was from the city, and he always dressed up
in something elegant. He seemed to talk
about nothing except law and order and
obeying the rules.

On Friday while Sister Ida was setting the table, she said to Jennie, "Just mind your manners while Mr. Cooper's here. No tricks."

"Sure," Jennie agreed. She knew exactly what was going to happen before the store-keeper even came through the door.

When Old Man Jenkins had built a new footbridge across Quicksand Branch, he had let the old one stand. It was so old and loose and rotted that it was about ready to go. Jennie had put a sign by the old bridge. It read, "Cross Here." Mr. Cooper always obeyed signs.

In a little bit they all heard some yelling
and splashing outside. There was the storekeeper thrashing in the water, with what
was left of the old footbridge floating beside
him. And when he dragged himself out of
Quicksand Branch, not only were his elegant
clothes a mess, but his wig had come off. The

28

storekeeper was bald! Nobody, not even Jennie, had known that. But when Sister Ida saw him, she said, "I think you look even handsomer without hair!"

Mr. Cooper was so relieved to hear that that when he was dried out some, he asked Sister Ida to marry him.

Zeph looked at Jennie and said, "What now, Jennie?"

The next morning Jennie's sisters were prancing around like young nanny goats. "Just think, when we go to the Ball, we'll all be engaged!" Sister Clara gushed.

Jennie said nothing. She just began to turn red.

Zeph sang softly, "Roll, Jennie Jenkins, roll!"

"What color fixups are you goin' to wear to the ball, Jennie?" asked Sister Ida.

"Don't know," said Jennie, pouting.

"I say you should wear white," Sister Clara insisted.

"The color's too bright!" Jennie snapped.

"She'd look good in blue," said Sister Fannie.

"The color's too true!" Jennie snapped again. "If it's silly answers you all want, it's silly answers you'll all get."

"How about red?" asked Sister Ida.

"It's the color of my head!" Jennie yelled.

"How about green?" Mizzus Jenkins asked.

"A shame to be seen," said Jennie.

Everybody laughed to hear that. "Well, how about yellow?" asked Zeph.

"Oh, that'd catch a fellow!" shouted Old Man Jenkins.

"I'll wear black," said Jennie.

"Black?" they all repeated.

"Sure, it's the color of my back!" said Jennie.

When they had stopped laughing some,
Mizzus Jenkins said, "Jennie, honey, what
will you wear?"

"I'll just go bare, Ma," said Jennie.

They could hardly sit in their chairs from
laughing so hard when they heard that.

Jennie stomped out. "Fixups!" she
snorted. "Fixups!"

"Roll, Jennie Jenkins, roll!" Zeph called
after her.

Jennie changed after that. She didn't get mad when Zeph hummed and whistled his tune at her. She smiled at everybody. And she surprised them all one day when she said, "I've changed my mind about the Nettle Bottom Ball. I'm lookin' forward to it. And I've decided on my fixups."

Mizzus Jenkins and Jennie's sisters were as pleased as flies on a hoecake. "We'll get started on your fixups right away," said Mizzus Jenkins. "You've only got a few days to get 'em ready."

"Ma, I want to ready my fixups by myself," said Jennie sweetly. "I know I can do it. I promise they'll be good ones."

So things got real busy around the Jenkins place. A day before the Ball Old Man Jenkins got disgusted and cleared out for the hills. Zeph was busy out in the barn running over all the fiddle tunes he knew. And Mizzus Jenkins and Jennie and her sisters were working on their fixups.

"What is the prize for best dancers to be?" Sister Clara asked Zeph at lunchtime.

"A hog all ready to butcher," said Zeph.

"I bet I know who'll win it," said Sister

FIRST PRIZE – BEST DANCERS

Fannie. "Brute Smith — no doubt. He's the best dancer hereabouts."

"Who's he takin' to the Ball?" asked Sister Ida.

"Nobody knows," said Sister Clara.

When the night of the Nettle Bottom Ball came, the storekeeper, Mr. Cooper, came to pick up the Jenkinses in his buggy. Preacher Jeremiah and Schoolmaster Tucker would be waiting for them at the school-house.

Jennie didn't go in the buggy. She wanted to put on her fixups last and ride to the Ball on Contraption. "We'll let her," said Mizzus Jenkins. "She's bashful. This is her first ball and she don't dance too good."

The Nettle Bottom Ball was marvelous to
see. The schoolhouse was filled with people,
and the decorations were something to look
at. The fiddlers were all tuned up and ready

and pretty soon the Ball was swinging along.
About the time folks were standing outside taking a breather from the first round

of dancing, Brute Smith came driving up with his huge wagon and a team of horses. He was all alone.

"Where's your gal, Brute?" people called out.

"She's a-comin'," Brute replied.

Then, with a great commotion, Jennie appeared on Contraption. She rode right up to the schoolhouse steps while folks scattered out of the way.

"I've come to dance up a storm!" Jennie cried, jumping off Contraption, who pranced and snorted at the sight of so many people.

But what a sight was Jennie! She was dressed in blue, white, red, brown, pink, black, yellow, green, and purple. There were stripes and polka dots and patches. On her head was a feather hat — chicken feathers, turkey feathers, duck feathers, goose feathers. People gasped. Jennie's sisters were horrified. Mizzus Jenkins cried, "Oh my, oh my!"

Jennie dashed into the schoolhouse.
"Clear the floor," she cried out. "I've come
to dance!" She turned and looked at the
fiddlers, especially Zeph. "No waltzes and
reels for me! Strike me up a jig!"

Zeph began to play the wildest jig he
knew, while folks crowded into the schoolhouse to watch. Brute walked up to Jennie
and said, "Those are some fixups. Let's
dance!"

Jennie and Brute danced like crazy. They whirled and stomped and shuffled and jumped and kicked until people got dizzy watching. Nobody else dared to dance with them. The young ladies, including Jennie's sisters, were as mad as bobcats. None of them could dance like Jennie, and it was plain to see all the men admired her. But after about an hour Jennie and Brute gave out. People

whistled and clapped and cheered for them, and it was agreed that they had won the prize for best dancing.

While Jennie and Brute were catching their breath and shaking people's hands, Zeph called out, "Folks, here's a new song I made up for my sister Jennie. I don't think she much likes it, but it's hers."

Zeph played his fiddle and sang the song he called "Jennie Jenkins." It was rollicking and funny and so much like Jennie herself that all the folks liked it and set to clapping.

"Thanks for askin' me to the Ball, Jennie," said Brute. "You're the only gal in these parts who don't seem shy of me. When you're more growed up, you and me will have to go to another ball."

"Nope," said Jennie. "I still don't favor fixups. That was my first ball, my last ball, and my only ball."

Then she jumped on Contraption. But before she took off, she grinned at Brute and said, "You keep the hog."

Brute and everybody stared at what they could see of Jennie disappearing down the road. Then it was pretty quiet, except for Zeph still playing softly on his fiddle and singing, "Roll, Jennie Jenkins, roll!"

Jennie Jenkins

A Traditional Melody
adapted and arranged by Mark Taylor

Oh, will you wear white, Oh, my dear, Oh, my dear? Oh,
will you wear white, Jen-nie Jen - kins? I won't wear white, For the
co-lor's too bright. I'll — buy me a fol-di-rol-dy - til-di - tol-dy,

Seek a dou - ble use a cause a roll the find me _____

Roll, _____ Jen - nie Jen - kins, roll. _____

1. Will you wear white, O my dear, O my dear?
   O will you wear white, Jennie Jenkins?
   I won't wear white,
   For the color's too bright,
   I'll buy me a fol-di-roldy-tildy-toldy,
   Seek-a-double, use-a-cause-a, roll-the-find-me,
   Roll, Jennie Jenkins, roll.

2. Will you wear red, O my dear, O my dear?
   O will you wear red, Jennie Jenkins?
   I won't wear red,
   It's the color of my head.

3. Will you wear black, O my dear, O my dear?
   O will you wear black, Jennie Jenkins?
   I won't wear black,
   It's the color of my back.

4. Will you wear green, O my dear, O my dear?
   O will you wear green, Jennie Jenkins?
   I won't wear green,
   For it's a shame to be seen.

5. Will you wear purple, O my dear, O my dear?
   O will you wear purple, Jennie Jenkins?
   I won't wear purple,
   It's the color of a turkle. *

6. Will you wear blue, O my dear O my dear?
   O will you wear blue, Jennie Jenkins?
   I won't wear blue,
   The color's too true.

*I.e., a turtle (turkle) dove.

DATE DUE